M000221006

Love Is a Hunger
Love Is a Necessity

Other books by Earnie Larsen

Days of Healing, Days of Joy
Stage II Recovery: Life Beyond Addiction
Stage II Relationships: Love Beyond Addiction
Old Patterns, New Truths

Love Is a Hunger
Love Is a Necessity

An Invitation to Grow

Learning
and Relearning
the Skills
of Loving Relationships

Earnie Larsen

**CompCare®
Publishers**

2415 Annapolis Lane
Minneapolis, Minnesota 55441
(612) 559-4800
(800) 328-3330

©1979 by Earnest Larsen
1991, second edition

All rights reserved.
Published in the United States
by CompCare Publishers

Reproduction in whole or part, in any form, including storage in memory
device system, is forbidden without written permission...except that portions
may be used in broadcast or printed commentary or review when attributed
fully to author and publication by names.

Larsen, Earnest.
     Love is a hunger, love is a necessity / Earnie Larsen.
        p. cm.
     Rev. ed. of: Love is a hunger.
     ISBN 0-89638-251-6
     1. Love. 2. Interpersonal relations. I. Larsen, Earnest. Love
is a hunger. II. Title.
BF575.L8L27   1991   90-19445
152.4'1—dc20   CIP

Cover and interior designs and illustrations by Pamela Arnold.

Inquiries, orders, and catalog requests should be addressed to
CompCare Publishers
2415 Annapolis Lane
Minneapolis, Minnesota 55441
Call toll free 800/328-3330
(Minnesota residents 612/559-4800)

   5   4   3   2   1
95   94   93   92   91

To Freddie

Contents

This book is a thanks to the chemical dependency unit at Mercy Hospital, Anoka, Minnesota, because a great deal of it came out of my involvement with the patients and their families.

Love Is a Hunger
Love Is a Necessity

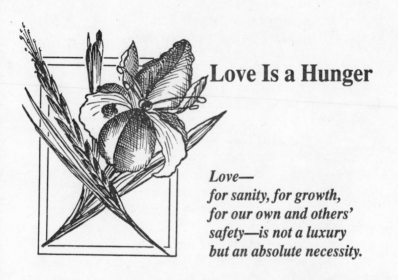

Love Is a Hunger

Love—
for sanity, for growth,
for our own and others'
safety—is not a luxury
but an absolute necessity.

Our planet is a huge, aching, pain-filled cry for love and loving; for being found and finding; for reconciliation and rebirth. Love is not a luxury, something just as well done without. Loving to humankind is like the heart beating, the mind thinking, the imagination creating exciting forms of beauty on the inner canvas of the brain.

Love is at the very center of who we are and how we are doing. Love is necessary. And—as it is with all necessities—when love is denied long enough, disaster follows, the world collapses. A primary objective of psychiatric healing—and often medical as well—is to lead the patient along the difficult but wonderful path of learning or relearning the skills of loving relationships. Every counseling session—either private or group—is a step along the line to learned love.

Bill and Jackie, as hundreds of thousands of other couples, sit in their counselor's office. Their marriage has turned sour. Automatically they say, "Sure we love each other but—." But there is no trust, no kindness. Their words are poisoned arrows, their attitude is "attack/defend." With the counselor's help, they will be led to a point of decision—a deciding whether to begin to try to love or not. To learn or relearn some of the skills of living together in love. If not—if these cannot be learned—if love is not born between them, if insights are not gained—they simply won't make it. The seed will have fallen on stone, and as all seed fallen upon stone, it will wither from lack of nourishment.

Dr. Glasser in his works—primarily *Reality Therapy*—says this spiritual nourishment cannot exist without what he calls "involvement." Viktor Frankl in his *Logotherapy* calls it "participation." Dr. Rollo May in his classic works calls it "community." All these are words for the skills and reality of shared existence, of dwelling together in harmony, of discovering beauty in and among ourselves and others.

Erich Fromm in *The Art of Loving* simply states that without loving relationships there can be no love. Without love there can be no health. Without health there can be only destruction. St. John calls this necessity of human living **love**, and Jesus plainly calls it the greatest commandment. Though in our everyday lives we all too often treat love or a loving relationship as a luxury, a dimension we can get along without, in reality we cannot; we either love or we die. And though there is but one way to live, there are a thousand ways to die.

Pat has not yet seen his twentieth birthday. Soon he will face the judge for dealing dope— narcotics. Pat refuses to accept acceptance. Those who love him open their doors wide; Pat has refused to enter. Unbroken by love, he demands to go it alone, to use others, to make nothing count but himself. He has never learned the skills of loving.

Joyce is fourteen. Somehow, in whatever way it happens, she has crossed over the line into negative-approval-collecting. The only way she functions is to make herself unacceptable. She sulks, tells everyone how bad she is, refuses to be happy, thrives on discord and misery. As of now she is cemented in negative living. A huge shell has built up around her. We can only hope, desperately, that it may crack open, as one of our own fights for survival.

When and if it does—if the shell disintegrates, it will be love, the gentle, relentless, stronger-than-violence power of love that will have made the difference. So far, Joyce knows nothing of love. She is untouched by its creative power.

Firm, gentle hand—or fist of steel? Acts of caring—or acts of violence? The difference is all a matter of love.

Sometime during that tragic struggle in Vietnam, somewhere in the Ninh Province, VC prisoners are huddled together. Their eyes show constant fear. They seem so small, so young, so defenseless there, eyes covered, hands tied. A thin American walks up to them. A strange light burns within him—a cruelty, a hunger, a demon. His name tells it all—they call him "Killer." Silently he waits. Eyes turn toward him. His fellow soldiers watch. He raises his rifle. Bones and blood fly in all directions. Killer is famous; he has murdered countless VCs. In that insane time, insanity seemed to be the only measure of normalcy. A month later Killer himself is dying. He lies in the arms of a young medic. A new kind of light now burns in him; the cruelty is gone. He tells the medic, "I never wanted to kill, never wanted to hurt anyone. It was only that I could do it well—the only thing I ever did that people said I was good at. They made me feel like a hero. I wanted so much to be special to someone..."

4

Love is not a luxury. In many different contexts, we say that love is the treasure above price, more excellent, more precious than gold or silver.

We say it, but our lives at times betray our lack of belief. It is love—not profit, or being right or strong or in control—that could reduce the number of those in "psych wards" and treatment centers, fill human hearts with the gentle sweetness that is a prime ingredient of sane living. Our outer world is only an expression of the mysterious, powerful, shadowy world of the inner spirit. If our world is filled with anger, hostility, distrust, then it is so because the inner worlds of all too many of us are starved and dying—starved of the harvest of love.

Thank God, thank Him a million times over for those people, those rare, precious, marvelous people who have learned the secret place and pitched their tents there. Those who dwell in the attitudes of hope and confidence, who reach across rather than down. Those people whose presence always leaves us feeling better about ourselves. Thank God for these loving people, these custodians of the secret of love.

Phil is such a custodian. The treatment center common room held maybe forty agitated people. This was the first, terrifying, hopeful, nervous evening of family encounter. Obviously there was a disease here, a killer disease that eroded trust, faith, and togetherness like waves washing away a beach. Eyes darted, hands twitched. Excited, meaningless conversation bounced back and forth. What would happen? The hurts had been so deep, the failures so frequent. Broken hearts and promises littered the floor like leaves in the fall. What would be the cure? Did someone have a magic answer, a remedy, a solution pulled down from the stars or dredged up from the human heart? Phil, the head of the treatment center, immense in kindness and glowing with some inner secret, slowly walked to the front of the room. He had been here so often, seen these faces, felt the desperation, knew the heartbreak. The restlessness ceased. The twitching stopped. All eyes fixed on his face. The expectation was ponderous. "We all have one hope," Phil said. "None of us can get well until we learn to love. That is what treatment is all about—learning to love."

He does indeed know a secret.

The Fountain

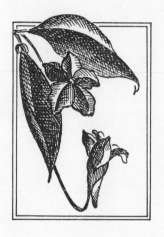

The human spirit can be likened to a fountain. The water filling the fountain is love. Notice, when things start going badly, when fights increase, when walls begin to rise obscuring the light of serenity, when cruelty bristles—very probably it is a time when the fountain is dry.

Love is not a single thing. It is made of many ingredients. Those ingredients fill the fountain. When a spouse begins to feel like a servant or merely one who brings home the paycheck, when the people in a supposedly loving relationship feel taken for granted, when gentle attentiveness ceases and trust evaporates, when priorities shift to other concerns, then the fountain becomes bone-dry. Then we had better beware: A time bomb starts ticking. Slowly the members of this relationship begin to feel alienated, cheated, alone—waiflike.

The daily tasks—even vacations that used to be such fun—these times of togetherness become chores. They find excuses not to be together. In some strange, unnamed way, there is relief when something comes up that allows separateness. The bomb ticks louder. In many subtle ways, each of these "waifs" makes his or her presence felt—painfully felt. Drinking no sweetness from the fountain, each has none to give the other. We learn to punish one another in such covert ways. Meals not prepared—or gotten home to—topics talked about, topics avoided, items bought defiantly, without consultation. Then what is covert becomes overt. When it is bad enough, when enough pain has been dealt out and received, help is sought—help to learn and relearn the skills of love, the attitudes of love. It is not a matter of indifference or secondary importance that the fountain is dry; nothing matters more.

The inner need for love and loving, for self-worth and participation in something more than self is indeed a hunger. As with physical hunger, it cannot be denied. No one is surprised when we concede that one who is starving will eat almost anything. Anything! Given enough hunger, the most delicate will fight for scraps. Hunger turned to starvation will make anyone capable of such extremes.

Spiritual hunger is no different. Endlessly it seems, the lines of demoralized, disheartened people pass through offices of all kinds, seeking help, drinking gallons of coffee mixed with tears, decrying what they are doing, what is happening to them, what they have fallen into. They seem so surprised, so shocked by what they have done. Yet a brief checking into the condition of the fountain, the depth of the waiflike feelings, the unrelieved ticking of the bomb quickly reveals a tremendous level of love starvation. They, too, are fighting for discarded scraps because they are so hungry. It is not a crime to be starving. It is only a tragedy to consume poisoned food when something so much more nourishing is at hand— or could be. The main point here, however, is simply to invite a measure of the level of the fountain. If we consider love a luxury and do not pursue its presence in our lives, do not actively invite it, put ourselves in the path of love, then like a bomb, our tensions tick away and explode, explode in ways that destroy our sanity, our growth, and very health. Certainly, there is the option to attempt substitutes. Facing the dry fountain, choosing not to deal with it, we can throw substitutes between the grinding wheels of life. Some of us stay busy—insanely busy; there are more than a few workaholics around. If one keeps busy enough, there is no need, no time or energy, to work on loving relationships. As young Joyce did, we can substitute negative action—anything to be noticed. Some may substitute a neurotic form of religion, one that takes them so far out of this world they never have to bother with it, as if they did not live on planet earth, crowded together with the rest of us. Toys can become a form of attempted escape. If only, we seem to say, I can get this other boat, new car, or several new dresses, **then** maybe I shall be happy, this gnawing hunger will vanish, this aching, empty fountain will finally be filled. But there is no substitute for love but love.

La Mancha

At one point in that brilliant play, *Man of La Mancha*, the visionary/hero is confronted by a "realist." But the hero, Don Quixote, chooses to live with a vision—a hope of what can be—to see the good that is around him.

His antagonist accuses him of not seeing reality, not seeing life as it is. Quixote responds with a question, what is life as it is? He has seen filthy bundles of humanity whimpering in the streets, men killed in war, poverty and starvation. Those elements are part of life. But there is more to life than that. We choose the world that will be ours. If we choose to accept and live in a loveless world, then that becomes "life as it is" for us. It is never a matter of indifference. If that becomes our choice, then the fountains drain dry, the waifs emerge from the far recesses of our spirit, bombs explode. We teach those around us, especially the children, that this is "life as it is." Expect nothing better. But it is so only for those who, lacking insight and skill, allow it to be so.

Love as a Relationship

In speaking of the crucial, vital dimension of human life, love, it is important to use accurate words and concepts. We often speak of "**having** love" or "**being in** love." This can lead to great confusion, even to harm. Love is the name of a relationship. It is something that happens between. These images—the fountain, the waif, and the time bomb—simply can't be understood except in the context of **relationship**. Perhaps another metaphor can be of service.

Most people, at some time or another, have enjoyed a circus. Most at least have seen circus acts on television. We know what a tightrope is. A tightrope is a line stretched **between** two poles. There can be no strong line, no sturdy rope if **both** poles are not capable of holding it up. There cannot be a one-poled tightrope.

Love is—in that sense—like a tightrope. It is a relationship stretched between, flowing between, existing between two poles, two people. It cannot be stronger, truer, more creative than both are willing to make it and capable of making it.

One person cannot take the full responsibility for a relationship. One person simply does not have that kind of power. If one pole, no matter how strong it seems to stand, is in a relationship with a facing pole that falters and falls, then there can be no creative relationship. If a rope is hooked to a fallen pole—no matter how strong the other support may be—it must lie flat on the earth. Dr. Martin Buber says it beautifully: "Feelings dwell in man; but man dwells in his love. That is no metaphor but the actual truth. Love does not cling to the I in such a way as to have the Thou only for its object, its content, but love is between I and Thou....Love is responsibility of an I for a Thou."

One cannot be too realistic when looking at the relationship of love, realistic both in the sense of where it can go (and there really is no limit) and also of where it is, of what it is. Fromm specifically called his book *The Art of Loving* because loving is an art. An art that must be worked at.

And to achieve a loving relationship, both must work at it. A tightrope can exist only between two poles. One can invite, hope, refuse to enable unloving behavior, but one person cannot take responsibility for the other. Exactly at this point is the gross risk of unfairness in loving relationships. One may be both willing and immensely capable of a loving relationship, hungering for it, begging for it, but if the other person is either unwilling or unable to be the opposite end of the relationship, then there can be none. Only increased misery flows from carrying around an unreasonable and mistaken burden of guilt if the primary relationships of your life are bone-dry and you insist (or get conned into thinking) it is all your fault. As long as the mysterious powerful flame or spark of love still burns it is imperative to try, to invite, to do all you can to break through the occlusions that prevent love from flowing, that keep the rope from stretching tight. But that is all one can do—invite. One person does not have the power to march inside the other, open the doors, heal the sickness, let in the sun. It is not only folly but dangerous to think otherwise. To be mistaken about the nature of love, about love as a relationship, allows anger, hatred, guilt, and the total loss of self-esteem.

Perhaps this point can be made clearer. Let us draw a three-columned page. On one side is the "I." In the middle are some of the qualities, the ingredients, that go to make up the jigsaw puzzle of love. In the third column is the "Thou," the other. It would look like the diagram on the following page.

I		**THOU**
_____	Trust	_____
_____	Honesty	_____
_____	Emotional Responsibility	_____
_____	Communication	_____
_____	A Sense of Freedom	_____

Just as an indication, a check list—mark the
percentages you feel each of you—first the "I"
and then the "Thou"—is contributing to the
relationship in each category. You may see these
percentages, at least by your estimation, as vastly
different. They very well may be vastly
different. And that is just the point.

As true, as achingly true, as it is that you can
only work on yourself, take the responsibility for
yourself, it is also true that a loving relationship
cannot exist except to the degree that both are
holding fast to the rope. To understand that is to
gain freedom from guilt and false expectations, if
the fountain is indeed dry or drying. It gives one

a much clearer picture of the nature of love. It indicates much more clearly the options available and the road to be taken.

As much as love is a hunger and a skill, as much as it is a relationship, it is also a process. There is no such thing as a static relationship. If it is not undergoing constant rebirth and growth, it is in the act of dying.

Love is always on the way. Where it is going is far more important than where it is at this moment. It is the process that counts, not just the moment. If a pole or both poles in a loving relationship have fallen but are in the process of being rebuilt, if both persons are relearning to trust and care, then no matter how long it takes, it is tolerable. For by and by they will "get there"—only to learn there is no such thing as a final "there." "There" is only "better and better."

But if the process is slipping away, moving apart, then there should be great concern. For just as there is only "better and better" in a process that is traveling love's precarious path, there is only "worse and worse" for a process going toward separateness.

What direction is it going? What are the percentages? What are the elements of the puzzle called love? We so easily say, "yes, we love one another but..." But there is no trust, no honesty,

15

no respect, no kindness. There is no specialness or attempt to make the other feel special. Then how can there be love? Where is its lovely face seen? When is its healing touch felt? Love is not a simple, single thing, but a whole maze of many elements, elements upon which the human spirit feeds and must sustain itself. Without these elements, time bombs explode and "bundles of filth" whimper in the street.

Trust

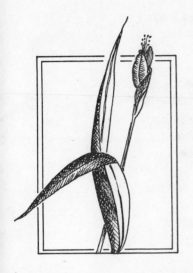

Trust is the certitude that the other person not only will not hurt me but is actively involved in the invitation of my growth.

There certainly can be no loving relationship, no tightrope, without trust. Obviously trust can mean many things, can apply to many levels. We can speak of trust as it relates to letting someone use a car or borrow a dollar. There are far deeper levels, however, where trust relates to more vulnerable personal dimension. But love is a matter of the utmost vulnerability and intimacy. What is written in italic letters here is both a definition and a description. It is a view of an element of love that can be tested in the model of the tightrope.

Trust is first of all a certainty. We might say it is a certitude in the guts rather than the heart, a feeling rather than a known fact. They aren't always the same. Someone we trust makes us feel very safe, very comfortable.

With the one we supposedly share a loving relationship, we know we should feel safe—but such is not always the case. Many obstacles block the way, people are taken for granted, efforts to identify and correct faults cease, self-centeredness sets in. Vulnerability is never risked or even thought of. Allowing love to **make us** diminishes to **making love** which degenerates to routine sex which becomes a mere function. What has happened to trust? Where is it?

There is only one way a feeling of certitude comes about—by something being repeatedly proven. We have certitude about the sun rising after it has disappeared in a beautiful sunset because it has always come back. We have experienced it happening. We can validate it personally. The only way we can be certain of trust is by others proving themselves trustworthy. If that proof, validated in our lived experience, is not there, no matter how much we want to trust, we cannot. Thus the model of the tightrope; trust is not merely a quality we each have separately but an element allowed to exist and grow between two poles. Trust is a sharing.

...will not hurt me

The first dimension of trust—call it a negative
dimension, but it is essential all the same—is the
certitude the other will not hurt me. I know that
because that person has not hurt me thus far. In a
real love relationship, chances abound for
hurting—for vulnerability is a piece of the pie—
but as often as those chances have arisen there
has also been proof of the credibility that the
other, the beloved, will not hurt me. And that is
why I feel safe, blessedly safe with that person.
Trust cannot exist in a win/lose type
relationship. If that process of the relationship
has flowed along the path that says one has to be
right and, thus, one wrong; one has to be smart
and, thus, one dumb; one has to be strong and,
thus, one weak; then trust has been murdered.

Often in the company of couples or "friends," if
you listen, you may hear the correction game
going strong. One says it is ten miles to a certain
place—the other offers a correction, saying it is
ten-and-a-half miles, to be exact. One says a
lamp cost fifty dollars, the other says it was fifty-
five. One says the event took place on May 17,
the other says it was May 16. As a matter of
fact, nothing can be said that is not corrected—
often with tones so sweet they drip sugar. The
real trouble is on the inside, in the realm of
emotional trust where there is no sweetness, only
hurt and hiding.

The I just does not really trust that the Thou is supportive.

Just as there is a fine art of loving, there is also an art to humor. Probably as much blood has been spilt by the mocking joke as by the sword. Minimally, trust means "You won't hurt me." Yet so often, in the name of humor, grave injury is inflicted.

We all have sensitive areas, such as how we look, what we have done, our opinions, what has befallen us. In the name of fun or even friendship, salt can so easily be rubbed into those sensitive areas. It might not be amusing at all when a wife jokes about the balding of her spouse. No more than when he jokes about how funny she now looks in her swimsuit. At a party or gathering, there may be gales of laughter—all in fun, of course—at a recounting of how someone backed into a fence, ran over a bike, and dented up the new car. But it isn't fun. Embarrassment runs high. Perhaps one is punishing the other in a subtle, but oh-so-effective way about damaging a new toy. It is not infrequent that when an embarrassing event has happened, perhaps even a minor tragedy, the victim is deathly afraid to be around friends, so low is the trust level. Losing a pet bird that flew away through an open cage door may be a minor event to one and a catastrophe to another. For the one to whom it is a catastrophe, it may cause

bitter tears. Trust vanishes when those tears are
ridiculed.

How often a "loved one" is held up to derision,
perhaps under the cover of a joke, perhaps not,
when one has struck out five times in a slow-
pitched softball game, had a flat tire and couldn't
fix it, lost a checkbook, missed a turn in the road
on a trip or forgotten to bring the sandwiches for
a picnic. No matter what the ridicule hides
under, the fact remains: when love and
sensitivity are lacking, when these hurting events
are dragged out time after time, a person can
bring about self-fulfilling prophecies—you **know**
the other will make fun of you, and it happens.
But when there is love, real love, one never
makes the other feel stupid or inadequate. Love
protects the other. Trust is that part of love that
knows the protection will always be there
because it always has been. Still, a minimal part
of trust is the acceptance that the other at least
cares about what I want. It is not just a one-sided
affair, in which the other always decides what
will happen, where we go, what we buy. Nor is it
always a situation in which "you decide—we'll
do whatever you want." Because you know that
isn't true; it is only a hiding place. For when you
decide, then if anything goes wrong, or if it is not
pleasing to the other, it's your fault, you come in
for the blame. These deeper levels of trust
always call into existence the reality of **we**. We
decide, we talk it over, for we are walking this

walk together. I trust that you will be there. I trust you will not only not go alone but will not hurt me if I attempt to come with you. Rising above the level of minimal trust is good, but it is not good enough for a loving relationship. If the relationship is in the process of rising above that minimal level—wonderful! It will get there. But with it must rise the certitude that one is also being actively invited to grow. Love is a journey, a process, a growth. Trust in love means not only that I am walking that journey but inviting you to journey with me.

The invitation to grow is always an invitation to rise above fear. Fear is the enemy. It is the "in spite of" that Paul Tillich clearly states stands between ourselves as we are and as we could be. In courage, we face the "in spite ofs" along our path of life and strive to do, to be, and to open up.

Trust—without which there can be no loving relationship—is the felt certainty that the other is actively involved in encouraging and helping me over these obstacles. This trust certainly can't exist if one is always afraid of being hurt by the other. Fear prohibits us from doing so many things. Locked up in many of us is a wish to write a poem, to make a table, to sing a song, to read a book, or to attempt some project we always dreamed of. Then why don't we?

More often than not the reason is fear. Fear of failure, fear of ridicule, fear of doing it alone. Trust is believing (because it **is true**) that the other will always encourage me to do what my dreams tell me. That other rejoices in my accomplishments, glories in my growth, invites rather than demands, encourages rather than cajoles, smiles rather than jeers. If I finally make something on a potter's wheel, that other proudly displays it in the house; if I finally join that discussion club, that person is anxious to go along with me or to hear what happened. If I make a good dinner or hit a home run in a game, there is cheering, not laughing. Trust is making each other feel good about ourselves and what we can do. People who don't make us feel good about what we do, and can do, we simply don't trust.

A deeper truth is that trust in what we can **do** has a profound bearing on our courage to **be**. Doing and being are not the same thing; nor are they totally separate.

In general, the more we discover we can do, the more we know who we are. The more confidence we possess, the greater the possibility of a sound, healthy self-image. In this second dimension of positive presence—deeper than trust to **do**—is the trust to **be**. Trust on this level is the loving affirmation of who we are. There is a great land-locked ocean in almost everyone, potential not yet discovered, not yet dared to be let out. There are words floating around that have not found the substance they fit; the words are ourselves—as yet unsung. Trust is knowing positively that the other wants those oceans to be undammed, those potentials actualized. This, of course, can happen in many ways but not without dialogue.

It is amazing how many people say "We love each other, but we never talk." There can be talk without dialogue (because nothing is said), but there cannot be dialogue without talking.

Two people I know—a couple greatly in love— have a room in their house called the quiet room. They have five young children; their house is a noisy place, but there is still a quiet room which exists because it is needed, just as the kitchen is needed. And this because love is needed and there can be no love without trust, and there can be no deeper trust without quiet talking. In a loving dialogue, planned and regular, we slowly learn it is okay to be who we are. And, in fact, to go beyond that and discover who we can be. Our others want that. They want it because our growth is important and because the more we are the more power we have to invite the others to be all they can be.

The kids slowly go to bed, the chores are completed, things are put away—quiet time. Vital, essential, quiet time. Time to listen and to speak, to reveal and be receptive, to get in touch with who we are and where we are going; to hear our song, what we have said to one another, and are saying.

In no other way do we ever come to believe we are worth knowing, in no other way do we ever trust that the other wants to know who we are and in return to be known by us.

This level of trust is heady wine. But so is love. The third level of trust in this positive vein, after trust to **do** and to **be**, is the trust to **open up**. Opening up has to do with vulnerability. The more we trust, the more we are willing to let others know who we are—our inner selves.

The deeper the journey, however, the greater the vulnerability. The more we trust, the more distrust slaughters us. The more the sacred qualities of trust in love are present, the more one can hear, in all that passes between the lovers, "Please, let me in." At first sound it seems confusing—let you in here? What do you want? You **are** in! Where else is there to go? But if the journey is genuine, there never is an end to the in-ness that is possible, possible only through trust. Trust, then, such an essential element of love, is the proved presence of one another. The certainty that I am safe here, I shall not be hurt. Far beyond that is the reciprocal trading of vulnerabilities. For two people to have trust between them, however, there must also be emotional responsibility.

Emotional Responsibility

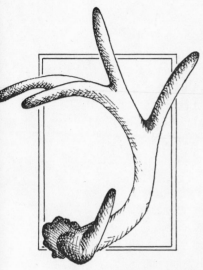

Emotional responsibility is the loving redemptive response to the vulnerability of the other.

The reason there is such a dearth of trust in loving relationships is because there is such a dearth of emotional responsibility. Trust and responsibility are a resonance. Neither stands alone in the context of a relationship—one is the response to the other. There is a soft call from the depths, depths of one to the depths of another. At one time the "I" is giving in trust, rendering the gift of vulnerability—at another time it is rendering the gift of responsibility listening to, accepting, receiving the vulnerability of the other. When one vital piece of the puzzle is lacking the whole puzzle is unfinished. The conversation has ended. There cannot be a conversation unless both persons are involved. If neither speaks—or both speak at the same time—there is no space between—it has been choked off.

The word "emotional" has been placed in front of responsibility for a major reason. All too often the word "responsibility" calls to mind merely physical responsibility. Frequently we will hear reasoning like "She's got a roof over her head. What else does she want?" Or "He has his meals cooked and his shirts cleaned; I'm doing my part." This, of course, indicates that the relationship is merely functional, that people are relating to one another only on a physical level, that humans are only physical beings. Certainly this is not the case. Spiritual and emotional responsibility are far more important. Obviously you can have deep, abiding love in a mud hut— and the very essence of hell in a castle.

The two dynamics to consider in emotional responsibility are the response and the invitation. Response has to do with the place of vulnerability in love. The precise response we are talking about is the response to vulnerability shared in trust. In all true loving relationships one doesn't love the pretense or masks of another person, but the other person. The more the one is able to say and share, "Hey, this is me, I don't have to hide or pretend," the more there is to love. The task therefore is to allow more of ourselves to be known. The process by which we allow that to happen—our own emergence—is

the process of increasing vulnerability. The
question in emotional responsibility is how we
respond to that gift.

The subtlety of this is enormous. I recall once on
a picnic—a lovely day—listening to a husband
try to encourage his wife to play volleyball. He
really wanted her involved. She thought herself
most unathletic and was greatly afraid to attempt
the game. She didn't trust. Patiently at first he
prodded her, explaining that there really was
nothing to it. The ball was big and soft. It
floated over toward her and all she had to do was
hit it back. She was afraid. Increased prodding
produced increased fear.

It all ended by him shouting, "Don't be so damn
dumb—all you have to do is stand there and hit
the thing." Needless to say, she never did.
I don't know if this couple have a quiet room.
I don't know if they ever speak to one another, if
they ever confide hurts and injuries. She was
afraid and force is never a solution to fear. At
first she was ready—hesitatingly—to try, but the
louder and more demanding the response, the
more she tended to hide, the more fear won.

The woman may never be a good athlete.
It doesn't matter. With enough emotional
responsibility, the couple can find much fun and
companionship, playing many sports. But she
was hurt, that part of her "I" which was

vulnerable on the volleyball court receded farther into the background, perhaps never to come forward again. There is less of her "I" to love—she will not allow herself to be seen.

We can be afraid of so many things, hide so much. Some people are afraid of darkness. For others this makes no sense. If the one trying to deal with this fear verbalizes it and is met with something like "Well, that's the dumbest thing I ever heard," the attempt probably will end.

Responsibility, like a broken bridge, had failed. I know a young man who is terribly frightened of heights. One summer working on a construction gang he was given the job of carrying out small buckets of cement to a swinging scaffold thirteen floors above the ground. The scaffold could be pushed out from the face of the wall, leaving only air under him for thirteen floors down. It became a great sport when trembling, faltering, terrified, he inched his way onto that scaffold, for the men to push the apparatus out, letting it slam back against the building. Such senseless cruelty passed as routine with this gang. What is not so obvious is that all too often similar cruelty passes as routine in our primary and secondary relationships. We simply cannot be trusting for long in the face of one who is not responsible.

The flip side of emotional responsibility is invitation. As it is **not** true that we are responsible for the decisions of another, not responsible for that person's growth or decisions, it is true that we **are** responsible for the invitation. An invitation is not a demand. A demand states that there had better be a response and an appropriate one, or there will be punishment. An invitation truly says "I would like your company. I ask for it. If you elect not to come that is your choice. I will not punish you for your way, it is yours to choose." Another way of saying this would be: We are not responsible for the door opening, but we are responsible for a gift being there, if and when the door is opened.

The practical application or at least the question this raises in relationships is—if we have a complaint that our others can't love, perhaps we should take a deeper look at whether or not they have been invited to love. If they seem so very uncreative and ordinary, perhaps they have not been invited to be any different. To such a surprising degree we are very much what we have been invited to be. In the process of straightening out marriage problems or any relational problems, it is a vastly different thing to sit back demanding that the other change than it is to be actively involved in the invitation for the other to change, to grow. One attitude sees the model of a loving relationship as unipolar. It says "When **you** change, then the rope will be stretched tight." The other recognizes the true nature of relationships in general and loving relationships in particular. There is no such thing as one pole not affecting the other and the rope between them. For one person to change—if the relationship is to continue—there must be the invitation from the other. Lacking this, there may well be a change, but the invitation will come from some other source. The response to healing and growth then will be to the source from which it came. Whatever the source, that will become the emotional center of the other's life. The call then from deep unto deep will be from that person to the other. One relationship will die; another will be born.

What is absolutely astounding in this often repeated phenomenon is that the very qualities found so lacking in one relationship are the same ones predominant in another. What has been born is not so much something that was never there as the qualities invited to emerge by a loving, concerned other.

"We love each other, oh, sure, we love each other—but..." But we never talk, never invite, never truly trust one another. And slowly the eagle that is in each one begins to fly in another sky. When that happens for a long enough time, there no longer is anything in common. The relationship has ended.

Just to see that love is a relationship and that all relationships are in process, going somewhere, is a healing in itself. It is a hope in itself. The emotional responsibility—both to respond to the vulnerability of the other in a loving, redemptive way **and** to invite the other to come out of hiding—is essential in the growing process of love.

However, the eye both of trust and emotional responsibility is honesty.

Honesty

Honesty is the conscious effort to eliminate games from my life and therefore from the relationships in which I am involved.

Honesty, like trust, admits of different levels. We can speak of honesty as not lying to one another, giving back change when we have been overpaid, returning a lost wallet. It is a far different matter, however, to be involved in the conscious pursuit of our dishonest games. There we are speaking not of honesty with others but with ourselves. Self-honesty is the willingness, fearlessly, to **look**. Without looking we really don't see, and without seeing we are truly blind. Without honesty, we genuinely can't know, or even guess, if we have been or are trustworthy, if we have been or are emotionally responsible. We don't know where we are—or where the other is—in the relationship of love. It gets all blurred, confused, mixed up. We don't know if we are dealing with our own games or others'.

Love is a relationship between an I and a Thou. Person to person. Facing one another. Games fuzz up what is going on. Games stand like dirty windows between the light of truth and who I really am, what I am doing, who the other is, what that person is. Dirty windows not only prohibit the light of truth from coming in, they also keep us from seeing out.

Hide the hatchet is a favorite game. What that means is—there has been a hurt, a misunderstanding, perhaps an instance of cruelty. The tightrope was not taut, the relationship was not healthy enough to talk it through. There was not enough trust or responsibility—so the hatchet was hidden. (But not hidden too deep, for it must be at hand.) A week or a month down the road something comes up—out comes the hatchet. Blood spills in bucketfuls. The hatchet-swinging has nothing, **nothing** to do with the moment. It is left over from the past injury—still unhealed. What can then happen is that the injured person tries to deal with the symptom.

But the symptom is not the cause. The cause took place months—or years—ago. What is being dealt with is **not** the issue. So nothing is healed. It is a deadly game.

36

If the game playing runs deep enough, is severe enough, there is not even the desire to name what is really going on. That, too, is part of the game. Not naming the problem makes it unhealable. You can never get to it. The hatchet goes in the back pocket again, awaiting another opportunity to jump into action.

Honesty is the conscious pursuit of the elimination of such games.

Another game that frequently obliterates the possibility of love, thus deadening our world, is "peace at any price." What this game says is that communication is too difficult. I do not want to face and name a situation that is killing me. So I deny it. I say it isn't there. I buy into the attitude of "peace at any price." The result, however, is that there never is any peace and the price is always too high.

One of the price tags—far too high—of this game is this: people, like relationships, are never static. People are in motion—they are becoming. The more we allow ourselves to tolerate the intolerable, the more we sanction and enable others to solidify their destructive behaviors. Then we are the ones left to live with those games. Then we are the ones who must increasingly blind our inner eyes to the destruction around us in order to survive. If that situation is not getting better and better, then it is getting worse and worse.

There can be a mysterious line inside a person, a demarcation beyond which there is no graceful coming back. Sometimes this is very visible. The eyes grow hard. The face never indicates what is really there underneath. Hostility replaces softness, walls replace doors. It is a tragic transformation to see. Truth seems to frighten these people, as though, if truth were embraced, it would be stripped away and the exposure would prove fatal. Once that line is passed and negativism sets in, any remedy will involve both time and pain. You can't push or rush these people, you can't coax or drive them (though they will take every bribe you offer). As good as you are to them, in your best efforts, they seem to relish hoarding up hatchets to chop down the very ones who love them most.

It all seems so senseless—the pain, I mean. Endless hours of counseling seem fruitless, for there seems to be no capacity for honesty, no truth, no vision.

Everything said gets turned around, twisted somehow. Alibis and excuses, often born of true genius, appear. There are no corners for these negative ones; they will not be caught. Obviously there is no easy cure or answer to such a common, tragic situation. But one thing is sure: The game of "peace at any price" is no answer or help. In fact, somewhere along the line that game—tolerating the intolerable, excusing and enabling irresponsibility—may have helped form a pattern.

In all Twelve-Step programs they speak of the elephant in the front room. Live long enough with that elephant, and you don't even know it's there. You accept it. Every night while reading the evening paper or watching the news on TV, you haul out the hay and water to feed the beast—it becomes part of the family. A visitor may drop in and be incredibly shocked. "My God," the caller says, "You have an elephant in your front room!" Our response all too often is "Where? I don't see an elephant." We don't even know it's there.

"Guilt" easily becomes a favorite game. We seem to be such a guilt-prone people. Guilt is easily used to keep people in line—just where we want them. If our attitude is not one of promoting their growth and happiness—truly **for** them—then we want them for **us**. We don't want so much what is best for them but what is best for us—what makes us look good or feel fine, even if it kills them. Take food, for instance: I know a physical fitness buff who exercises constantly. He believes excess pounds are the scourge of the world—not only his, but anyone else's as well. His wife is not fat, nor is she a physical fitness buff. The man loves the way he looks; he doesn't love the way she looks. In his mind she makes him look bad. Guilt becomes his weapon. He makes her feel horrible if there is a cookie around the house. He asks her what she ate when she went out with her friends. Never in an angry, hostile, accusing way, but quietly—with a smirk and sneer. Tension is like a killing smog around their house.

He innocently says, "I want her healthy, I don't what her to die of a stroke or something." He is the good guy, she the bad. She says that isn't true. What he is most concerned with is how she looks when she is with him around his friends. The obvious point is—they don't trust one another. Trust is absent because responsibility doesn't exist. Nor can it without honesty.

Guilt truly can control people, but love is not a matter of control. If controlling is the goal of "love," as understood by one of the two, real love can never exist. If he puts on enough pressure and she buys into "peace at any price," she may shrink to a shadow. But there will never be love. It was demanded—not invited. As the fountain dries, the waif stands out more starkly, the hunger increases. The body may have stopped eating, but the spirit rages on. A substitute will be found, something at least to ease the inner gnawing. That substitute may well be poison. Somewhere along their lives' path a counselor or doctor may ask them, "But what went wrong? What happened? How did you end up like this?" And blind eyes may look from tanned faces in utter bewilderment. "I don't know—I really don't know."

Love is not a luxury; it is an absolute necessity for sanity, health, growth, and safety.

Prophets

A prophet's job is to tell—or foretell—the truth. Prophets come in all forms. Each of us needs our own tellers of truths, our own prophets. The trouble is, we often kill our prophets because we don't really want to hear the truth. With healthy attitudes between us, we can be prophets to one another. We can talk to one another. We can ask for others' visions, for their perspectives, their views.

"This is the way it seems to me, how do you see it?" It seems so simple yet it is not. For such a question demands that we listen and **want** to hear. If we are involved in some game or other that is casting ruin around us, it is vital that we listen as the others speak. It is vital that each of us has someone, that we each allow someone in our lives that we can **and will** ask. If we do not have our prophets, who is left to tell us the truth?

It is not important here to offer an exhaustive list of games, dishonest ways we deal with one another. The point is that without honesty and the desire for honesty, the conscious pursuit of it, we don't know the games we are playing. With our inner window thus dirtied, we don't know or recognize the games being played with us either.

Love, being a process, can certainly tolerate slow growth, the climbing out of dishonesty; but it cannot tolerate willed dishonesty. Love flies on the wings of communication. Willed dishonesty breaks the very wings that would carry us into the heavens.

Communication

Communicating indicates passing through the point of pain to deeper understanding.

The sign simply read, "The only way out is through." It could have hung anywhere. This one hung on the wall of a treatment center. Its truth is endless.

Frequently when arriving at a hard place, a place full of pain, we don't go through; we try to go around. We go around by ignoring the problem, calling it by another name, dealing with the symptom, confronting someone who has nothing to do with the problem.

Communication is the act of going through. And that act is always the result of a choice. We

choose to want to communicate or not. Of
course, again—communication takes two; it is a
decision both make. But once made, the
mysterious, marvelous, magical insides of both
the I and the Thou are able to know and be
known. Hiding stops. Energy that was spent on
running to escape is now expended on revelation.
We want to know each other as we really are and
are becoming, what is behind the things we do,
what old patterns we wrestle with. Will we go
back to being waifs?

A waif is one who feels left out, used, not loved;
one who has a feeling in the pit of the stomach of
what it's like to stand outside a warm, lovely
store window with not a dime to spend, shoes full
of snow. Feeling like a waif is a sickness, a hurt.
It is easily healed, however, at least temporarily.
To heal the waif, it takes a loving arm around the
shoulder, or a sincere "How are you? Want to
talk?" A hand held out, an invitation to join in—
be part of the crowd. These things are what it
takes. How often have we seen the lone wolf,
scared, hurt, alienated, standing alone, spewing
hurt and pain to all around become absorbed in a
totally different reality when invited in.

Into love, into the group, into involvement with
them. Every conversation story ever told, every
situation of one ransomed, redeemed, is the story
of a waif who found home; of a yellow-eyed
wolf wandering the back timbers of

consciousness who finally found a way out, and in that loving invitation lost its claws and fangs, lost its desire to tear and rip, lost the urge to fight. Only estranged waifs deported to the fringes of love need respond to their world with anger, violence, and hostility.

Love is not a luxury.

At times all of us feel the waif in us. Some, because of past experiences or tender personality, feel it much more than others. When the waif is in control, either there is communication or there is disaster. Now here is the problem: For most it is extremely difficult to say, "I feel so alone, rejected, left out." The reason, of course, is because of fear, lack of trust, lack of responsibility. It is hard to ask "Please, love me." The temptation is to act out all sorts of other games, get irritated about the weather, moan about supper, complain about the cost of living. It gets worse and worse. But communication is the word, the act of passing through the point of pain to a deeper, more genuine understanding of who we are as individuals and as poles supporting the tightrope of a loving relationship.

If we are communicating, one can say, "The waif is in control," trusting, knowing the other will gently say, "Let's talk about it." Perhaps it was something done, a single act or a series of minuscule events that alone amount to nothing but collectively become mountainous. Very possibly it was a misunderstanding, something wrongly interpreted. A look assumed to mean "You bore me," or "Why don't you stop saying such dumb stuff," or "You sure do silly things." Did that look **really** say that? We suppose, but we don't know. True, it is risky and painful to say "Is this what you meant?" It is a crossroads of pain. Communication is the act of facing, and then passing through together, that crossing, where there is a stumbling block or stone in the road.

Once friends, lovers, couples, or groups have faced such crossroads of pain and passed through, they can have the surety that it **can be done**. Communication is possible. On the wing of such surety trust is born.

Of course the waif feeling is but one kind of moment, one point of pain. There are many. There can be conflicts over money management, time expenditure, manners, politics, religion—a list without end. There never will or can be a time in the process of building a loving relationship when points of pain are nonexistent. Love is not free. The price we pay is our willingness and ability to pass through those points of pain, whatever they may be: we emerge, perhaps scarred, but deeper and better for the passage.

There is an alternative—not a happy one—to communication, just as there is an alternative to love. What often is substituted for genuine communication is fighting. Fighting becomes the elephant in the living room, familiar, comfortable, accepted. When it becomes accepted, however, again it becomes a self-fulfilling prophecy. When points of pain emerge we just know "we are going to have a fight"— and we do. But there are other options, infinitely preferable to cruel, demeaning fighting. Fighting, with all the verbal abuse that often goes with it, as in the case of all violence, is a proof of failure. Violence in all its forms is the expression of powerlessness. As long as we feel there is power to handle a situation in some other way, we do not resort to violence. Violence is the ultimate failure. Not only is there all too often fighting in lieu of communication, but often it is said that fighting is good, a necessary release. Cruelty is never beneficial. There are creative ways of dealing with rising emotions—anger, disappointment, resentment—but they may well be painful. If we understand fighting to mean the crash, out of control—the burst of emotion, often dishonest to the core—then there is no good in that. It is a retreat that must be made up if the relationship is to continue. Supposed lovers and friends can become accustomed to fighting.

They glibly say it is no big deal. But this should not be said too quickly. Trust is a very nebulous

47

quality, fragile for all its strengths. Fighting often brings out angry, hostile words and emotions, and trust is violated. This is not to say that friendships don't continue, that one avoids the company of the other. But all too often there is not as much openness, not as much invitation. No one likes to have a tender spot rubbed (even if the rubbing is in the name of a good-natured fight) or to be subjected to violent abuse.

The pain is still there. It still hurts. And we are less likely to expose that tender spot again.

Some have even said it is good for kids to see their parents fight. It gives them a taste of "reality." What reality? It is far better for children to see adults encounter points of pain, potential battlegrounds, and handle them in a creative, loving manner, than it is to witness violent scenes of disrespect and injury. Children are defenseless against their environment. If they live with models of hurt and injury, then these do indeed become their reality. What a precious gift to offer children—the knowledge that there is a different reality than abuse: **found-ness**.

Communication comes from two Latin words which, when combined, mean to build a wall together. It means pulling side by side—as partners. Perhaps more in our age than in any other, there is a vast, gloomy, hideous fear of being alone, isolated and alienated. The prospect of not having an other, of having no one to pull with you, lies at the root of innumerable cases of both mental and physical illness. We are not made to live in isolation. Yet so many of us find ourselves right there, alone and un-found.

In communication, we experience the exquisite sweetness of being found. We dared to say, "This is the real me," as though we were saying a password before a menacing gate, and the response was "Enter." How we hunger for home, for a place to belong, to come into and rest. How worth the effort not to end the journey at a point of pain, but to pass through—to reach out a hand, perhaps into the darkness, into distrust and doubt, but reach it out all the same, asking someone to respond and together, hand in hand, journey on. The price is high, the risk great, but the reward is greater.

When communication is sincerely sought and achieved—for in sincerely seeking we are communicating—we arrive at another most essential piece of the puzzle of love. That is, we discover for certain that the others seek only to set us free, not to possess us.

A Sense of Freedom

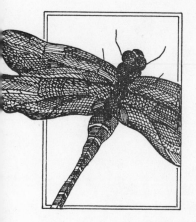

Only those individuals who have chosen to lean without losing their individuality can participate in a loving relationship.

Love is a necessity, not a luxury. As with every necessity there is a "have to" attached to it. There is no "have to" with a luxury—that is why whatever it is is a luxury. A necessity at the heart of love is for both persons, both poles, to retain their integrity as individuals. Individuals are persons who can truly say "I." These are my tastes, opinions, likes and dislikes—this is what is negotiable and this is what is not. There is an "I" here who has the power to make choices, to decide, an "I" who will listen, consider, evaluate, but then will take the terrifying risk to say, "I choose, I decide."

It is true—as it has been repeatedly said in these pages—that love is a relationship. It does not reside in one pole but exists in the space between. It is true that for love there must be a pulling together, a common building; but there must also be a distinct "I" or there is no pole. It is not within the nature of love that one pole of the relationship becomes or allows itself to become a mere shadow of the other.

One part cannot become a blotter that absorbs anything poured before it. It is paradoxical, but not contradictory, that love demands two, but each one of those two must be at least on the way to being a true individual. The rope stretched between the poles falls when one person attempts to own or dominate the other, when one must be slave to the other's master, one dumb to the other's smart, one wrong to the other's right. Only free individuals are capable of free decision. Regardless of the risk and fear, that springs like some protective shield in a science fiction movie when the thought of setting someone free emerges, it must be done. If I **have** to love you I can't. No one can love by **having** to. I can be forced to render obedience, service, time, but not love. So often when the spark, the sweetness, has gone out of a loving relationship the outer manifestations have not changed; there still are the same meals, the same routine, the same vacations and parties, but something vital is missing. What has died is the free choice, the decision, the **want** to that can only be when you know, in trust, the other wants you to be the best **you** you can be. For that **you** is the only you there is to bring into your relationship. The attitude of love is not to possess but to set the other free.

Once free, a person can then choose to lean or to walk alone. Love is leaning. It is the choice to lean. What does it mean to "lean"? On one hand to "lean" means to risk, to allow ourselves to need each other.

Our world would not be the same without each other. That difference goes far beyond physical or monetary considerations. Emotionally there has been a rooting process going on, a coming together, a melting. When we lean, we are as willing (if perhaps not always as able) to share a weakness, a fault, or a fear as we are a strength, a success, or a victory. Leaning means being willing to turn oneself inside out in the presence of the other, so that all that is beautiful can be celebrated and all that is broken can be tended to. The attitude of leaning was tenderly portrayed in the award-winning movie, *Rocky*. He had gone the distance, all fifteen rounds. In his own way he had won; he was the champ. It was his moment in the spotlight.

People pushed and crowded around; they wanted his attention, his words, his thoughts and emotions. But Rocky had learned to lean without losing his own identity. He wasn't nearly so caught up, absorbed, carried away by all the adulation as he was desperately looking for his Adrienne. He wanted her, to share this moment with her, to bring her into the spotlight as well.

He didn't want to be there, glamorous as it was, alone. The sweetness of their coming together would never have happened if they had not, all along, also shared their fears, their hard times, their doubts and disappointments. They had risked when, in their vulnerability, each could have been devastated by the other. So now they could also share, by leaning, the thrilling ecstasy of victory. On the other hand, leaning is more than just risking vulnerability, asking the other to be there for you. It is also the "summum bonum," as Robert Frost called it, the greatest good one gives another in love.

In our production-oriented world, our efficiency-minded, perfectionistic, get-the-job-done society, it is extremely difficult not to be influenced wholly by these attitudes. When one of us chooses to lean, however, in a loving relationship, trusting that the other is asking us to lean as well, we are not talking about earning or production or job ratings. What one member in a loving relationship always says is: "First of all, lean; first of all, need me; first of all, in our individuality let us be One. Then, then we can deal with all the rest. But first of all, let us lean."

All too often our response, if ever we find ourselves in such a situation, is much like Tevye's wife's in the play *Fiddler on the Roof*, when he asked her if she loved him. Embarrassed, taken by surprise, she started to spout a thousand stammering things she had done for him, things they had done together during a life lived many years side by side. But these weren't answers to Tevye's question. Those were functional answers to a spiritual question. His response was along these lines: "Yes, I know all those things; that isn't what I am asking. What I ask is do you love me? Are we more than living side by side? Are we also together? Has the melting wax of our lives flowed as one, making a third and new reality that can never be the same if one departs, that in fact never can be taken apart?" "Side by side" we live legally; "together" involves the spirit.

The invitation to lean does not, first of all, say, "Make a lot of money, be an expert cook, never get old, play with the kids, be handy with tools, love to discuss what I like to talk about." All of those may well be important for our loving relationship, but first of all something else must be considered: First of all, let us lean, as two cards supporting and holding one another up. If one falls, so does the other—not in the sense that the individual goes under but that the relationship is broken.

By leaning—strange as it may seem—we set our others free because it is a recognition of their worth and importance in our lives. Leaning obviously calls for a decision and a risk. The decision is about what is really important; the risk is that if one decides the relationship is the number one priority and the other doesn't, there is heartbreak ahead. And yet the sad fact is: If the relationship is not number one something else must be.

From time to time, there have been random polls taken concerning "the most important thing in your life." The answers, as you can imagine, range all the way from having money or success to saving one's soul. Each answer, of course, is open to wide interpretation. However, if the relationship, consisting of both poles and the "rope" between, is not of primary importance, then it will suffer, possibly collapse. Would it not be fascinating to give the persons in any loving relationship a chance to express what each would perceive as the number one priority in the relationship as well as the number one priority of the other?

Granted that in such instances there is often discrepancy between what is said and what is lived, this could offer insight. Possibly there might be such items on the list as golf, hunting, playing cards, or walking with friends, spending money, church.

How many people, how often, would put as first "helping the other, the one I love, to know that he or she is number one in my life, that our relationship, our being together, is most important to me, for that is what I have chosen"?

Without that attitude being present, there is immense danger of the dry fountain, the waif-feeling, this ticking bomb exploding.

It is our choice about what is number one to us. Yet how easy it is to slip into the attitude of "I can't help it." It's not my fault the golf league meets so often, or the bridge club decided to play so frequently. It's not my fault the job is so demanding. Or the schedule ended up like it is. We may not choose a situation but we **do** choose what we do with it. It is our choice how we respond to it. It is our choice what we make or allow to be or communicate as most important.

Nor does it make much of a dent to say "It's all for you." Seldom home, working all the time, involved in countless charitable projects "all for you." But what the other, or others, may well want is not all the things money can buy, but presence, the presence of the one they love. It may well be that, no matter how often a person says "It's all for you," what the other really hears is that whatever it is that takes that person away is far more important.

Number one priority, leaning, setting the other free—all these can be communicated in countless ways. No relationship is exactly the same as another; therefore the symbols used in communication are never the same. What is an absolutely essential symbol to one relationship may not be to another. But the inescapable truth is that however it's said and lived, however it is communicated, a person is aware of being "number one" or special to another. He or she knows it. And when that person **isn't** "number one" or special, he or she knows that, too.

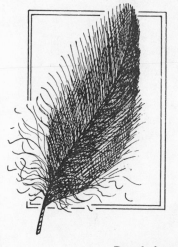

A Feeling of Specialness

Specialness is the attitude of tender respect extended to another, an attitude that says "You are unique and precious to me."

People love in a lot of ways. Symbols differ. The manner of exchanging love symbols may differ greatly. For some, dressing up and going out is vital to the maintenance of the relationship. For others, it is as foreign as Mars. Some relationships thrive on gentle teasing; others don't. Some are filled with gifts of flowers, cards, notes, or poems; others count on jokes, fish fries, and ball games. The music of some genuine relationships is classical, of others—just as real—country and western. Some relationships are comfortable in jeans and tank tops, others in evening gowns and suits. Some couples ride in jeeps and pickup trucks, others in limousines. Some go to the opera, others to drive-in movies. Some indeed may include all of the above at different moments. But no matter what the manifestation, how it is expressed, if it is genuine, if there is real love between two persons, if each is standing even stronger and straighter in individuality, there is always the nebulous but very real element of specialness, each to the other. The two involved know beyond doubt that they are special to one another. Each knows he or she is precious in the heart and sight of the other. On this point of regarding each other as precious or special, we can be very careless. Under the guise of "We have been married too long," or "He (or she) knows; I don't have to break my back proving it," or "We are beyond that stage," it is very easy to let preciousness tarnish, to allow specialness to disintegrate. We may be communicating to the other an attitude of disinterest that says, "You or another—it really doesn't matter." Here comes the elephant, snorting and blowing, grudgingly accepted, living in the front room. We can say what we will about it: "It really doesn't matter," or "The little things don't count," but they do. Lacking the mutual regard of specialness, all that is left is the waif-feeling and the empty fountains and the ticking time bombs.

Specialness, however, is an imponderable. It is not concrete and is even less able to be expressed in any kind of percentage than honesty or trust. If trust has been broken, dishonesty slipped into, situations can be named, incidents brought up, events remembered. Specialness, the quality of being precious to another, or regarding another in a special way, is more elusive than that. It has to do with the kind of care often present at a time of birth or death, at a time of tragedy or serious sickness. At those times a special light burns in the hearts and faces of those present. There is a glow, the glow of concern and caring for someone precious. Signs of affection abound. Extra phone calls, just to see how the loved one is doing, become automatic. The tone of voice drops, the harshness often dissipates. There is not so much coldness or insensitivity. A hand seldom grasped now reaches out to hold and be held. Communication is happening. The message: You are special to me, you are precious. My world is not the same without you. In fact I dare not even think of my life apart from you. I may not know well how to say it, show it, I am not a poet or a troubadour, but my heart is trying to tell you you are precious. Seldom is the message not heard. The main key to communicating preciousness is not to be a poet or a troubadour but to **want** to communicate it. And you can only want to if it is true. What is tragic is that it often is true but it doesn't get said. We wait, thinking it unimportant, trivial, "not my style"—wait until it is too late for one reason or another. The train has pulled out and left us behind.

Every genuine loving relationship has that about it which breathes specialness and preciousness. These attitudes automatically give birth to respect and beauty. These, too, are imponderables, scarcely—if at all—able to be measured, weighed, evaluated. But there is no problem in recognizing when they are present, or in feeling the hurt when they are absent.

Respect—like the bald eagle—is endangered. For many reasons, partly social, partly economic, partly based on personal experiences, we hardly know what respect is. We are taught so much to use things, use them and when they are worn out or no longer useful to throw them away and get new ones. Some of the world around us is indeed to be used but much of it is to be met. Not used. They are not the same.

In order to "meet" a segment of the world, whether it be human or not, we must have an attitude of quiet receptivity. We must be able and want to listen. We must desire not to possess or capture, but to allow ourselves to be captured by it; we must not want so much to wrap it up and take it home as to ask it—be it music, art, poetry, or a human relationship—to allow us to merge with it, to touch us, to accept us as guest and partner.

Notice in any art museum—any that has truly fine art—before each of the best pieces there is a bench. Some think it is just a place to rest. A place to sit down between looking at pictures or statues. Not so. Sensitive viewing of art requires proper distance. From too close a vantage, the magic of the masterpiece is lost; the whole is lost in too close a scrutiny of the parts. From too far away, again the masterpiece is lost, for we cannot see well enough the harmonious interaction of the parts making the whole. The benches are not randomly set, much less are they just resting places. They are purposely placed at the proper distance from the work in front of it so we can see it from the best distance and angle, look at it reverently, hear and understand its message. Nothing can be heard or seen without respect, without proper distance. There is no art greater, more God-like, more healing, more important than the art of building, maintaining, and fostering loving relationships. Though the symbols and manner of expression may vary, the needs for respect, quiet, specialness, and preciousness are essential.

Johnny is a young man, a Greek-god young man, who loves motorcycle racing. It is a rough, dirty sport. When it rains, mud and slush are thrown around by the bucketload. In summer's roasting heat, bikes and riders take a terrible beating. People become passionately involved in this sport. They care. Between races, Johnny always props his bike up, takes out a rag and cleaning fluid, focuses his mind and lovingly tends to his

bike. As much dirt and dust as possible are
rubbed off. Parts are oiled, filters cleaned, nuts
and bolts tightened. Were the bike a human
being, it would surely **know beyond doubt** that it
is loved. Often things like motorbikes, rare coins,
stamps, flowers, and animal pets of all kinds—
were they able to know—would know heart-deep
how they are loved, respected, cared for, while
countless persons could not even guess anyone
would miss them if they died on the street. It is
indeed a strange thing to ponder how people who
can expend such love and special regard for all
sorts of inanimate and living things find it simply
impossible to express the same gentle concern for
another human being. Hours can be whiled away
cleaning and oiling a favorite rifle, but scarcely a
moment spent fondly caressing the face of a
beloved. It is killing to be second place to a rifle,
or a bankbook or a snowmobile or anything else.

Respect and regard for preciousness and attitudes
bloom like flowers whenever beauty is seen.

But then beauty is never just seen—beauty is
always entered into. As the symbols of love
differ, one person's beauty is not necessarily
another's. I know a man who could dream of
little more beautiful than the boxing skill of
Sugar Ray Robinson. It was ballet, poetry, and
the primal excitement of the battle and hunt—all
rolled into one. Someone else might see only
brutality there.

The point is that when whatever or whoever presents beauty to us—beauty which we grasp and allow to grasp us—feelings of preciousness and respect rise immediately in our hearts. A fierce desire grows to protect and preserve, to enhance and allow life. We feel the dual sensations of pride and humility—great pride, for in the face of beauty we always are proud; humility, because in the face of great beauty we always seem so small, so honored to be there.

We find delicious, exciting beauty in polished wood, fast horses, delicate flowers, masterful craftsmanship on dishes, guns, iron work, in the writing of a poem or the painting of a picture. Because we find beauty there, our attitude changes; manners soften, our spirits deepen. In the presence of a celebrity we find beautiful or powerful, we can scarcely find our tongues. We stammer and stutter, perhaps make no sense at all. The celebrity knows we are impressed, knows he or she is something special in our lives, knows what power he or she exerts over us.

But does not all love make of those involved celebrities? Can there ever be love without the sense of beauty, giving rise in its discovery to feelings of specialness, preciousness, and respect. True, living close to the celebrity may erode that person's beauty in our eyes, but if that were to happen, then the power would be gone, the specialness erased. That person would just be ordinary then, like everyone else, no one special. When that happens within a relationship called love, when there is nothing special left, when there is no respect or regard for preciousness, the poles fall over, the rope lies on the ground. The fountain dries up.

There may well not be more important words in a relationship than "please" and "thank you." We can say "I love you" when we have to, but if we have not also said all along "please" and "thank you," how much can love be believed? When a person asks "please," it acknowledges the need to ask, not demand. It admits that the relationship—the togetherness with another—is a gift, not a right. One tells the other, "I come as a poet, not a pirate, I ask to be let in, I seek permission to enter." Then "please" becomes a sweetness stronger than force, a binding tighter than chains. It is a word of a guest, not a crusader. "Please" says, "I know you don't have to, but I hope you will." "Please" is a word used in the face of beauty, of specialness and preciousness. Its absence clearly says, "I find no beauty here, nothing special." Courtesy, politeness, manners—no matter how crude or unpolished—always, invariably accompany a sense of encountering the beautiful. And if a beloved is not beautiful, can they be beloved?

"Thank you" indicates that a gift was given and recognized as a gift. It was not a debt repaid, a right rendered, a law fulfilled. Gifts are more than that. Gifts can only be gifts when freely given. But what was merely a right rendered can bloom into a beautiful gift when met with a "thank you." Not just a surface sign of social compliance, but a genuine "thank you" from the spirit, acknowledging our poverty, our inability to be the same or do as well without the gift of the other. "Please" and "thank you" state clearly who the other is, what the other means in a loving relationship. They say volumes about the other's degree of specialness and preciousness in our eyes, about the appreciation of beauty, the awareness of the quality of giving involved in all relationships. Love is a necessity. For health, sanity, and safety, we need to know we are special, precious, beautiful in the sight of those who love us. Were we all to know that, to feel that, we would see in marvelous quantities the visages of demons change before our eyes into the lovely faces of angels.

The Angel
and the Demon

*Love and also the lack of love
are powers. As with all
powers, love is neutral.*

Power itself is neither good nor bad, creative nor
destructive. The outcome of power, its effects on
our lives and world, depends on other factors.
Consistently throughout these pages, we have
stated our main premise: Love is not a luxury—
it is a necessity. The power within each of us—
reaching, raging, rushing to find its connection—
wears the face of the angel if integrated into a
loving relationship. If not, it wears the
multitudinous face of the demon. What is most
helpful to understand, as with the model of love
as a relationship, is that the need for love and
loving relationships is power.

Power is either an angel or a demon depending on what we do with it, on how well we handle it.

The truth about power is that, again, it is like a rope having two ends. We might call either end of this rope of power the angel and the demon. Looking at this model of the rope, however, it becomes obvious they are not two different things—they are but different ends of the same rope. If we cut off one end of a rope, it will still have two ends. What must be done is that the whole rope must be placed in a context where it will be beneficial to everyone.

The difference between a Hitler and a St. Francis was not simply that one was bad and one good, one a Saint and one a killer—the fundamental difference was that both had immense power, yet one integrated that power into a whole, healthy personality; the other allowed the power to become uncontrolled. Hitler no longer possessed the power, the power possessed him. The famous thinker Rainer Maria Rilke put it simply: If you kill my demon, you also kill my angel. If you put out the fire, true, no one can burn down the world, but neither can the fire light the darkness or warm the chill off a freezing night.

The question we face as individuals and as a society is not simply how to kill all those elements that so militate against love and loving relationships. The demon cannot be killed any more than one end of a rope can be cut off. The quest is not one of killing, but of integrating the power, of channeling it, so that the form of the angel appears rather than the gargoyle shape of the demon. Anyone who reads these pages thoughtfully, using them as mirrors and as check lists for the direction of that vital element, love in our lives, no doubt will find room for growth. These pages were written in the light of the ideal, the goal to be strived for, the growth to work toward. There is no such thing as perfect love or perfect loving relationships, because there is no such thing as a perfect human being. People are flawed. We cannot be perfect; we can only work at progress.

Whatever these pages lead us to, personally or relationally, as areas for growth, we can face them and say, "I'm going to destroy the fear, selfishness, and apathy that drains the fountain and saddens my world with waif-like feelings." But the demon can only die if the angel becomes stronger.

It is one thing to say "I will be less afraid"; it is another to say, "I will allow someone to walk with me in my fear." It is one thing to say, "I will be less self-centered"; it is another to say, "If I allow my fountain to be filled more often, I will have much more energy and willingness to fill the fountain of another." It is trying only to kill the demon without recognizing the true nature of power to say, "I will stop nagging," without also saying, "I will allow myself to be held." Only people who feel good about themselves can be part of a loving relationship. That gift of improving self-image is partly a gift to ourselves which we acquire by putting ourselves in the way of it, recognizing its importance. But it is also a gift we must give to others. Each is a mirror before which the other stands. If all one sees reflected back is an inadequate, stumbling, not-good-enough partner, then what else can the other do but agree? And thus agreeing, there is nothing else to give the other. The mirrors become so distorted they are incapable of mirroring back the beauty that is truly there.

Making love work, however, does not depend simply on killing the demon. It is not so much a matter of fasting and doing penance as it is a matter of feasting on the God-like qualities others can offer to us. We have such a tendency for seeing the world shallowly, as divided into opposites, good and bad, right and wrong, night and day, beautiful and ugly. Beneath the surface, however, these opposites are related, affecting one another, flowing back and forth. Little progress can be made if only one is seen.

Dr. Rollo May has done extensive work on this question of the angel and the demon. He uses the term "demoniac," which is a Greek word translated into English as "genius." "Genius" is

the strange, peculiar, mysterious power
emanating out of certain people we call geniuses,
those who have special communication with their
own inner selves and thus with the gods.
Regardless of what all else genius may be, it is
power, inner power seeking a release, seeking to
express itself. When this genius is present along
with the talents of a Rembrandt, Michelangelo,
or Einstein, the results are visible and profound.
To a lesser, but not less important degree (at least
for us), the same process of genius seeking
release is unfolding in each of us. For someone
to reach out respectfully, lovingly, and take the
hand of a beloved—just to hold for a moment—
might for that person be as great a release of
personal, inner power as Raphael found in
painting his Madonnas. That gesture may be as
much an expression of who the person is and is
becoming as any work of a great master. That
same power, however, if not integrated in a
loving way, if not involved in a creative kind of
release, can also guide the hand that in anger
strikes the children, breaks the furniture, or runs
the car off the road. The question is not one of
who is good and who is evil, it is fundamentally
a question of how individual power is being
channeled.

Dr. May explains with dramatic and greatly
helpful insight that what we are talking about
here is demonic possession. Not as in *The
Exorcist*, but whenever an emotion such as anger,

fear, resentment, or jealousy runs out of control, paralyzing our lives and becoming the sole concern of consciousness. Then there is a type of possession in process, one that must be dealt with or exorcised. He uses the context of a primitive exorcism among jungle tribes. The external situation is different from our own, but the inner dynamics are not. He recounts the tale of a man possessed by hatred and resentment, in a country that occupied his land. The possession had come to dominate his life.

The rite of exorcism followed these steps:

1. The man came to admit the obsession.
2. He "embraced" the possessing demon by putting on a uniform of the hated enemy. Thus, he "wore" the demon that possessed him.
3. In the company of the rest of the tribe, he acted out his hatred.

He danced, sang, threw himself around. All through the ritual, his clan, his friends were there to support him, to comfort him and urge him to continue until the demon was integrated, replaced by the angel of tolerance.

Another incident Dr. May tells about had to do with a man's hatred for his mother. She had dominated him totally, ruined his life up to the present. The man desperately wanted to be free of the possession.

The same steps followed:

1. He first of all admitted the possession.

2. He put on the dress of his mother.

3. He underwent the same ritual, wrestling with
   the demon in the company of the tribe—
   always in the company of the tribe.

Dr. May states very clearly that this would be
impossible to undertake alone. Our demons are
too terrifying to confront alone. Exorcism must
always be carried out in the presence of
supporting people.

As bizarre as these events may seem, the
dynamics remain constant in our own time.
There can be no escape, no exorcism, from the
demons of fear, hatred, resentment without first
of all naming what is in control. There can be no
healing or deepening of love and loving
relationships without first of all being willing to
see where things are, to answer a check list of
some kind, to peer into a mirror. When the truth
is seen, a decision is made—always. Will I
admit and deal with the overweight problem, the
drinking problem, the loneliness problem? Will I
embrace it, face it, put it on as a uniform or
dress? Will I wear it, grasp it from the inside
out? Or will I deny it? As a patient who is dying
may, until the end, deny the stage of the disease
which is robbing him of life. The denial may
indeed take place, but it changes nothing about

the dying. If the decision is to embrace the offending demon, this, too, must be done in the company of a community—friends, family. And then comes the wrestling, the turning this way and that, the running and hiding only to face it again and return to the arena.

Earlier we spoke of a treatment center scene—where forty or fifty people gathered together to wrestle with demons, to transform demons into angels, to learn to love. There an angel-filled man spoke the words of truth and life, "The only hope for all of us is to learn to love." Those may well sound merely like pretty words, poetical words and thoughts, devoid of the stuff of harsh reality. Those familiar with redemption and treatment know such is not the case. For many in that room, the angel will be too fearful, the support too weak, the skills too fragile. The truth will not be faced, the struggle not undertaken, the exorcism not finished. The demons of wall-building, fear, apathy, and dishonesty will not be transformed into the angels of vulnerability, trust, enthusiasm, and gentleness.

But for others whose time is right, whose time is now, the slow passage will begin to take place. Something so real it defies words will begin to happen deep within the temple of self; there will be **a shifting**. That which was thought indispensable for survival will be discarded. Huge pillars will begin to be moved.

Faintly at first, then with more and more clarity,
like a sunrise, there will be the daring to think, to
hope, to invite; something really can be different
this time, it can be better.

Self begins to glow like an electrified orb, like
the brilliant sun, and in that glowing, the other in
the relationship wakes to life as well. One
glowing initiates a response on the part of the
other. Deep calls unto deep. The call is heard
and answered. Poles straighten; the rope of
relationship stretches in creative tension. An
intricate switch opens new tracks; a new way
becomes accessible to travel, ugliness is
exchanged for beauty, the fountain fills. The
waif, so long familiar, passes from cold into the
Eden-like warmth of specialness. A miracle has
happened, the world is better, much better, for
this one magical, marvelous event: that which
was lost has been found.

About the Author

Earnie Larsen is a big, gentle man with an ability to touch the hearts of all those who have accepted the challenge of creating change in their lives. He has authored more than forty books and produced audiotapes on a wide range of topics—from managing interpersonal relationships to spirituality. As a pioneer spokesman for the addiction/recovery field, he has developed important guidelines for what he has identified as Stage II Recovery. A nationally applauded presenter and seminar leader, he speaks, often to standing-room-only audiences, about getting well and staying well—about creating healthy relationships, healing from family dysfunctions, moving from anger to forgiveness, building self-esteem, and the importance of spirituality. Earnie Larsen has an M.R.E. degree in theology and education from Loyola University of Chicago. He has a degree in counseling with accreditation in chemical dependency and family counseling from the University of Minnesota. He has been counseling youth, adults, and families for over twenty years.